D0975990

Dedicated to my fucking wife.

Contents

Fuck

HOW TO
SWEAR

An illustrated guide

Stephen Wildish

CHRONICLE BOOKS
SAN FRANCISCO

First published in the United States in 2018 by Chronicle Books LLC.

First published in the United Kingdom in 2017 by Ebury Press.

Library of Congress Cataloging-in-Publication Data is available.

ISBN: 978-1-4521-6776-3

Manufactured in China

10 9 8 7 6 5 4 3 2 1

Chronicle Books LLC
680 Second Street
San Francisco, CA 94107
www.chroniclebooks.com

Chronicle Books publishes distinctive books and gifts.
From award-winning children's titles, bestselling cookbooks,
and eclectic pop culture to acclaimed works of art and design,
stationery, and journals, we craft publishing that's instantly
recognizable for its spirit and creativity. Enjoy our publishing
and become part of our community at www.chroniclebooks.com.

Introduction

Introduction

When executed correctly swearing can
be a true artform, a thing of beauty,
a way to diffuse pain, or insult a colleague.
Perform it incorrectly and prepare
to make an ass of yourself.

"UNDER CERTAIN CIRCUMSTANCES PROFANITY PROVIDES A RELIEF DENIED EVEN TO PRAYER"

Mark Twain

"OH FUCK, I SAID SHIT… OH SHIT I SAID FUCK!"

Queen Elizabeth

Devices for Creative Swearing

POETIC DEVICES

Metaphor
"You're a dickhead"

Simile
"You look like shit"

Alliteration
"Bloody bollocks"

Rhyme
"Fuck a duck"

EXCRETIONS

Fecal

"A piece of shit"

"Shithead"

Urinary

"Piss off"

Bodily Organ

"Asshole"

Devices for Creative Swearing

ACTIVITES

Suggest that the person engages in an unsavory activity

"Go fuck yourself"

Eat a bag of dicks!

Incest

"Motherfucker"

Sodomy

"Bugger"

Fellatio

"Cocksucker"

Bestiality

"Sheepshagger"

Swear Words Ranked by Severity
from MOST to LEAST likely to Offend

CUNT
FUCK
TWAT
SHIT
ASSHOLE
DICKHEAD
WANKER

BOLLOCKS
BASTARD
ASS
PISS
BUGGER
BALLS
CRAP
BLOODY
GOD

LEAST LIKELY TO OFFEND

A Brief History of Blasphemy

The term profane is derived from the latin **profanus** meaning **outside of the temple**.

Offensive swear words change over time according to cultural attitudes towards God, sex, and excretions.

For most of history, it has been considered highly offensive to utter God's name in vain or to mock the traditions of the church. It would have been very unusual to hear someone say "oh God" or "bloody hell." Phrases that are now commonplace.

Although fairly respectable before, the main expletive of the eighteenth century was **bloody**. It was heavily tabooed during 1750–1920. **Bloody** was controversial until the 1960s, but the word has become a tame expletive or intensifier.

Current taboos are for sexual acts and excretions (words that were commonplace in past centuries).

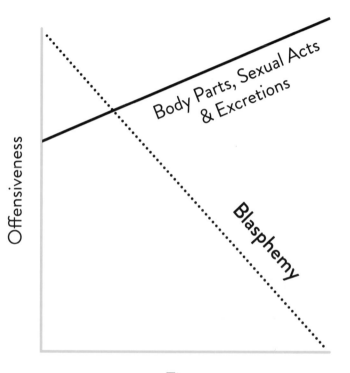

Offensiveness

Body Parts, Sexual Acts & Excretions

Blasphemy

Time

Building an Effective Insult

By adding a rhythmic **fuck** and an additional adjective, you can build an effective insult from a baseword. On the example here we have the added bonus that you can expand the word **dick** into **dickhead**. Most body parts can be expanded in this way (e.g. **ass** expands to **asshole**).

Nicely fucking done!

Expand on any remaining words
(e.g. dick becomes dickhead)

Order of Adjectives in Insults

Adjectives in the English language follow this order:

OPINION

SIZE

AGE

SHAPE

COLOR

ORIGIN

MATERIAL

PURPOSE

The same is true for insults . . .

Correct order

"You stupid, little, old, fat dickhead"

Incorrect order

"You old, fat, little, stupid dickhead"

Correct order

"You smelly old twat"

Incorrect order

"You old smelly twat"

Chapter 1

$$\{Fuck\}$$

Fuck

A word with origins in the act of sexual intercourse. One of the most versatile words in the English language, it can be used as a noun, a verb (both transitive an intransitive), an adjective, an interjection, imperative, conjunction, or an adverb. It can also be used as an interjection and a grammatical ejaculation.

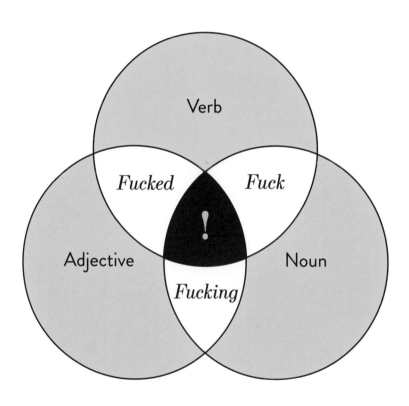

Etymology of Fuck

There are many theories about the history of
the word fuck, some more convincing than others.
Here are two of the most widely circulated:

German Roots

Fuck has similar roots in German words like **ficken**
(to fuck) or the Dutch word **fokken** (to breed).

Greek Roots

The Greek word **phyō** has several meanings,
including to beget or to give birth to.

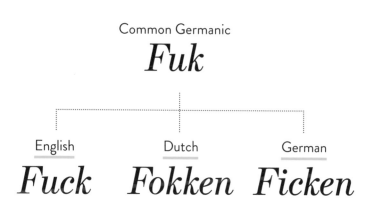

Common Germanic
Fuk

English	Dutch	German
Fuck	*Fokken*	*Ficken*

You gave birth to a stupid fuck!

Fuck as an Adjective, Verb, Noun, and Grammatical Ejaculation

Adjective

"Fucking fuck!

Grammatical ejaculation

Adjective  Verb

The fucking fucker's fucked!"

Noun

Correct use of Fucking as an Infix

The correct use places the infix in the middle or the first half of the destination word.

Correct

"Abso-fucking-lutely"

Incredi-fucking-ble!

"Absolut-fucking-ly"

Incorrect

Correct Use of Fuck as an Intensifier

The correct use places the intensifier toward the end of the phrase. Addition of the definite article can be required.

"None of your business"

"None of your fucking business"

"*Shut up*"

"*Shut the fuck up*"

Conjugation of Fuck

This is where the word fuck excels. Fuck can be placed before most pronouns, creating varying meanings.

Subject	Object	Number	Gender	Person
I	Fuck me	Singular	-	1st
You	Fuck you	Singular or Plural	-	2nd
He	Fuck him	Singular	Masculine	3rd
She	Fuck her	Singular	Feminine	3rd
It	Fuck it	Singular	-	3rd
This	Fuck this	Singular	-	3rd
They	Fuck them	Plural	-	3rd

Fuck...
- *you*
- *her*
- *him*
- *them*
- *it*
- *this*
- *that*
- *all*
- *off*

Acceptability of Fuck and Fuck Derivatives

It is not advisable to use the word fuck in front of vicars or children. Therefore, use one of the examples here. All can replace the word **fuck** or **fucking** (e.g. *oh for fudge sake, flipping heck!*). How far you go down the chart is for you to judge based on the occasion and the stuffiness of the guest you wish to "feck off."

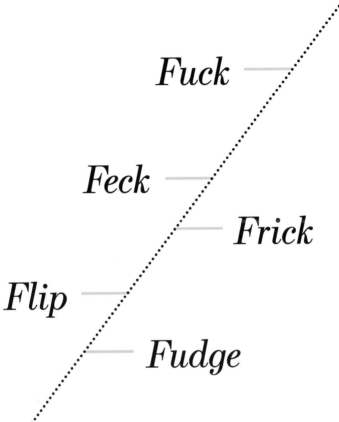

Offensiveness

Motherfucker as an Adjective and Noun

Noun

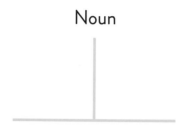

"*Motherfucker, you fucked…*

Verb

…my motherfucking mother"

Adjective

Fucking Senses

Literal sense

"Fuck me"

Figurative sense

"Fuck off"

Personal sense

"You fucker"

Fucking Tenses

Tense	Meaning	Example
Simple past	He did it	He fucked
Simple present	He usually does it	He fucks
Past progressive	He was doing it at that time	He was fucking
Present progressive	He is doing it now	He is fucking
Past perfect	Before that time, he had already	He had fucked
Present perfect	He has done it already	He has fucked
Future	He will do it	He will fuck

Passive

FUCK ME FUCK IT FUCK THIS

Aggressive

FUCK OFF
FUCK YOU

The F Word

The power of fuck is such that it is often referred to as **the F word**. There are only a few words bestowed with this honor (or dishonor).
The F word has also been used to ironically refer to feminism, as a pejorative homophobic slur, or, worst of all, a TV show about food.

THE F WORD

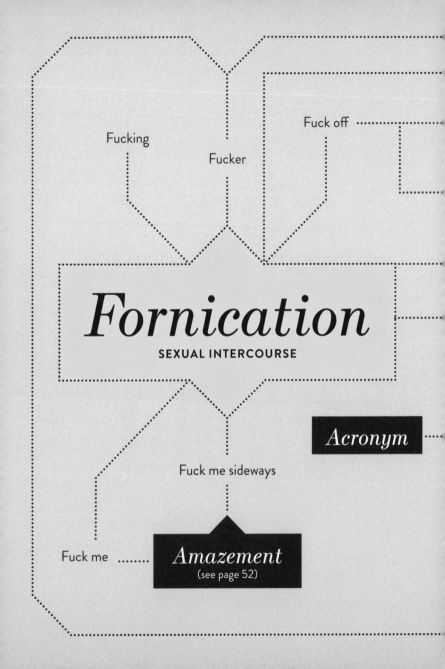

Fucking

Fucker

Fuck off

Fornication
SEXUAL INTERCOURSE

Acronym

Fuck me sideways

Fuck me .... *Amazement*
(see page 52)

Go fuck yourself

Abuse
(see page 51)

Fuck off and die

Fuck you

Motherfucker

MILF
(Mom I'd like to fuck)

Epithet
(see page 50)

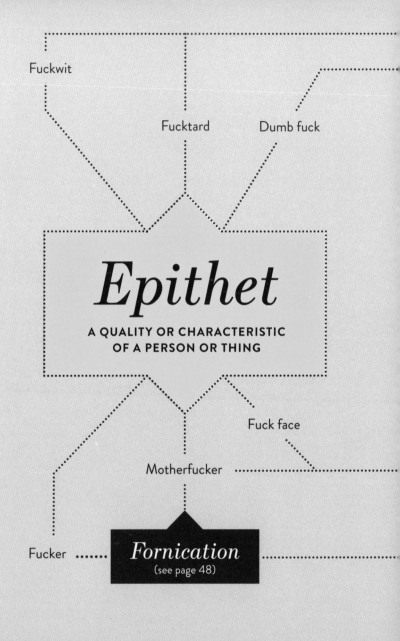

Fuckwit

Fucktard   Dumb fuck

Epithet

A QUALITY OR CHARACTERISTIC OF A PERSON OR THING

Fuck face

Motherfucker

Fucker

Fornication
(see page 48)

Feck

Get to fuck

Abuse

PERSONAL ATTACK

STFU
(Shut the fuck up)

Fuck off and die

Go fuck yourself

Acronym

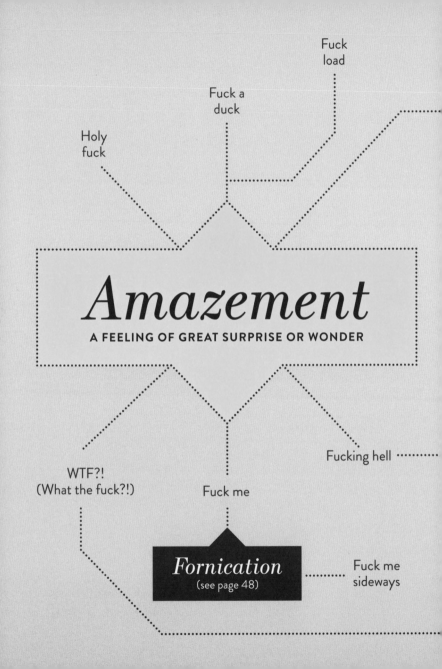

Fuck
load

Fuck a
duck

Holy
fuck

Amazement

A FEELING OF GREAT SURPRISE OR WONDER

WTF?!
(What the fuck?!)

Fuck me

Fucking hell

Fornication
(see page 48)

Fuck me
sideways

Fucking A!

Celebration

HONOR OR PRAISE PUBLICLY

Fuck yeah!

LMFAO
(Laugh my
fucking ass off)

Resignation
(see page 55)

Acronym

Acronym

FUBAR
(Fucked up beyond
all recognition)

SNAFU
(Situation normal:
all fucked up)

Tired/Broken

FUCKED

It's fucked

Fucked up

I'm fucked

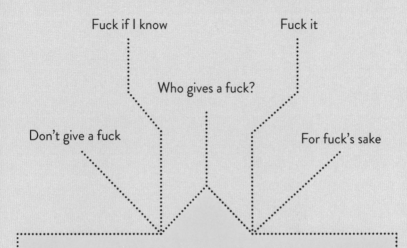

Fuck if I know

Fuck it

Who gives a fuck?

Don't give a fuck

For fuck's sake

Resignation

**ACCEPTANCE OF SOMETHING UNDESIRABLE
BUT INEVITABLE**

Fucking hell

Amazement
(see page 52)

Chapter 2

{Shit}

Shit

Although as a noun, shit refers to fecal
matter, it has many additional meanings;
to defecate, something of little value, nonsense,
or as an expression of surprise, or anger.

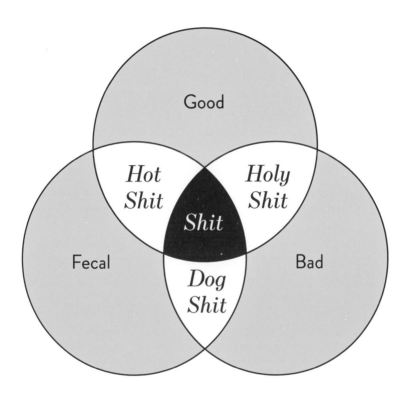

Etymology

The origin of shit is shrouded in the steaming mists of time, possibly derived from Old English, which had the nouns: **scite** (dung) and **scitte** (diarrhea).

This eventually changed in Middle English to **schitte** (excrement), **schyt** (diarrhea)

The word has several similars in modern Germanic languages:

German: **scheiße**   Swedish: **skit**
Dutch: **schijt**   Icelandic: **skítur**

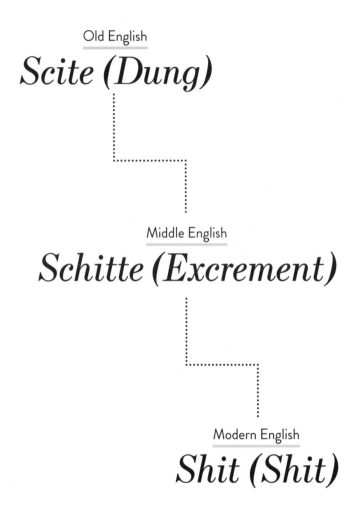

Old English
Scite (Dung)

Middle English
Schitte (Excrement)

Modern English
Shit (Shit)

Punctuation

KNOW YOUR SHIT

OR KNOW YOU'RE SHIT

Shit as an Adjective, Verb, and Noun

Adjective

"The shitting shit…

Noun
(person)

Verb
(to defecate/feces)

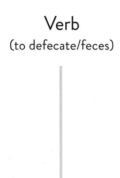

...shat on my shit"

Noun
(object)

Good shit

THIS IS GOOOOD SHIT

Bad shit

WE ARE IN SOME DEEP SHIT

Animal Shit

Adding an animal before the word shit
can vastly change its meaning.

Chicken shit = **Cowardice**

Dog shit = **Rubbish**

Apeshit = **Anger**

Bullshit = **Nonsense**

Horseshit = **Nonsense**

Batshit = **Crazy**

I'm bloody livid!

"Apeshit dog"
A mad dog

"Dogshit Ape"
A very poor excuse for an ape

Tenses

Tense	Meaning	Example
Simple past	She did it	She shat
Simple present	She usually does it	She shits
Past progressive	She was doing it at that time	She was shitting
Present progressive	She is doing it now	She is shitting
Past perfect	Before that time, she had already	She had shat
Present perfect	She has done it already	She has shitted
Future	She will do it	She will shit

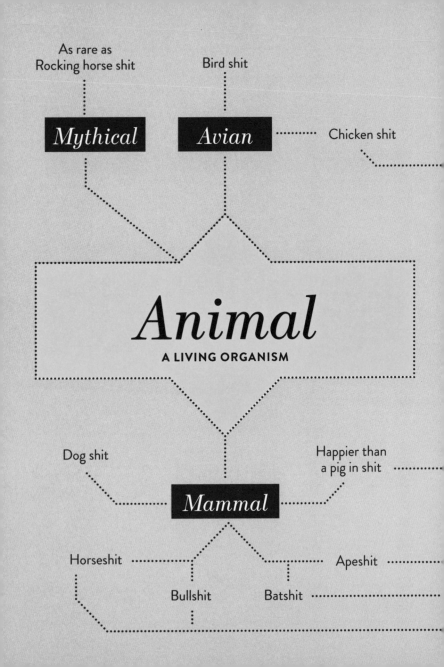

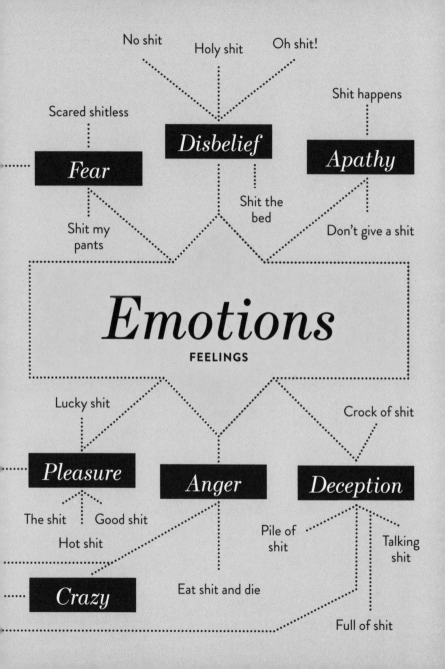

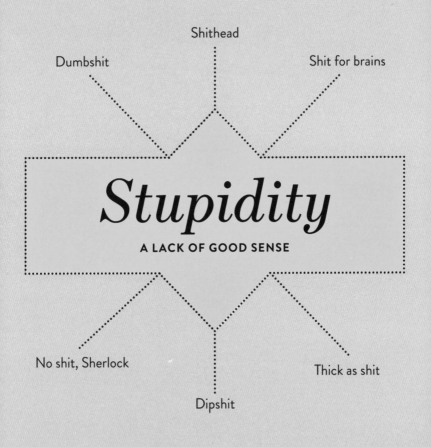

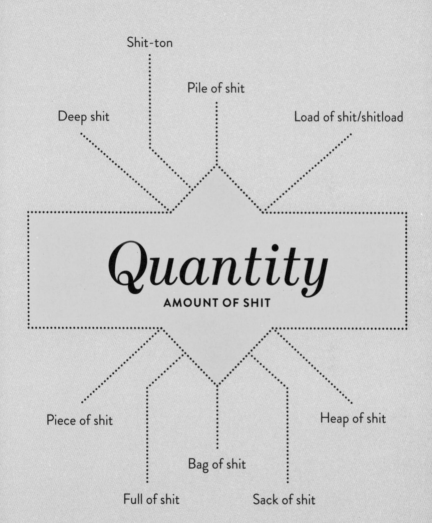

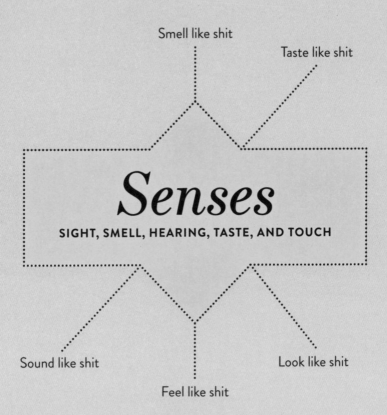

Smell like shit

Taste like shit

Senses

SIGHT, SMELL, HEARING, TASTE, AND TOUCH

Sound like shit

Feel like shit

Look like shit

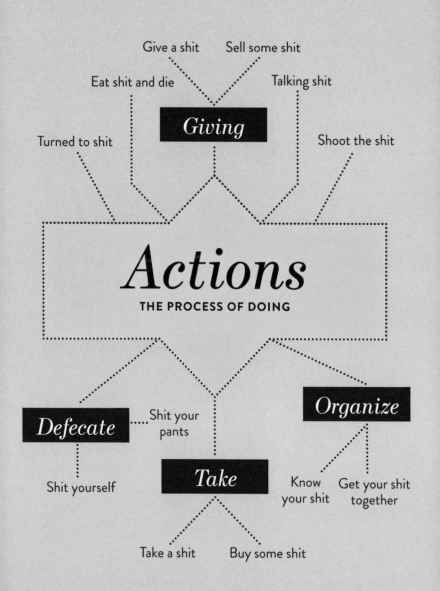

Shit Creek
without a paddle

Shit out of luck

Deep shit

Bad News

AN UNWELCOME DEVELOPMENT

Shitstorm

Oh shit

Turned to shit

Chapter 3

{*Piss*}

Piss

A slang term for urine, a sterile liquid
produced by the kidneys of many animals.

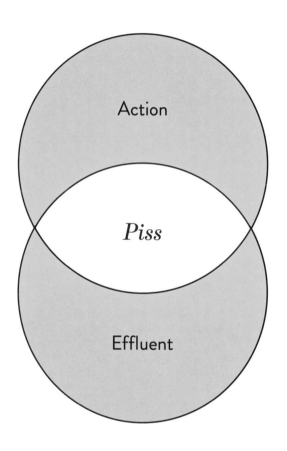

Etymology

Piss comes from the Old French word **pisser**.
Both words are onomatopoetic for the
sound of urination. Mostly used before the
fourteenth century, before being replaced
with the more clinical term, **urinate**.
Piss is now considered a vulgar term.

Old French

Pisser

Modern English

Piss

Piss as an Adjective, Verb, and Noun

Verb

"I'm pissed off—it's...

Verb  Noun

...pissing down with pissy piss"

Adjective

Context

As with many vulgar words, context is everything. If we take a phrase like **pissed all over it**, it could mean that you literally urinated over an item, or figuratively that an activity was very easy, or you have a superior skill or talent.

This tea tastes like piss!

Literal Sense

Urinating over an object

"Pissed all over it"

Urinating in your clothes

"Pissed myself"

Figurative Sense

The activity was easy

"Pissed all over it"

Laughing

"Pissed myself"

Tenses

The grammar around piss and its tenses is more complicated because of the three central meanings of piss (being drunk, being angry, and urinating).

	Past	Present
Verb	Pissed	Pisses
Participle	Pissed	Pissing

	Tense	Meaning
I was pissed	Past	Intoxication
I was pissed	Past	Anger
I was pissing	Past	Urination
I am pissed	Present	Intoxication
I am pissed	Present	Anger
I am pissing	Present	Urination
I will be pissed	Future	Intoxication
I will be pissed	Future	Anger
I will be pissing	Present	Urination

Easy

PIECE OF PISS

Hard

PISSING IN THE WIND

Pissed all over it

Piece of piss .... **Easy** ....

Difficulty

RELATIVE EASE TO COMPLETE A TASK

Hard

Plaiting piss

Pissing in
the wind

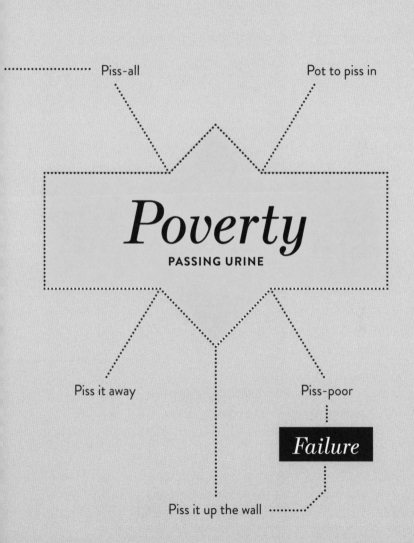

Piss-all

Pot to piss in

Poverty
PASSING URINE

Piss it away

Piss-poor

Failure

Piss it up the wall

Anger
(see page 97)

Pissed as a fart

Pissed as a newt

Pissed off

Drunk

BEING PISSED

On the piss

All pissed up

Piss up

Pisshead

Piss artist

Insults
(see page 96)

Cat's piss .... **Animals** .... Rat's piss

Beer

ALCOHOLIC BERVERAGE

Tramp's piss .... Warm piss

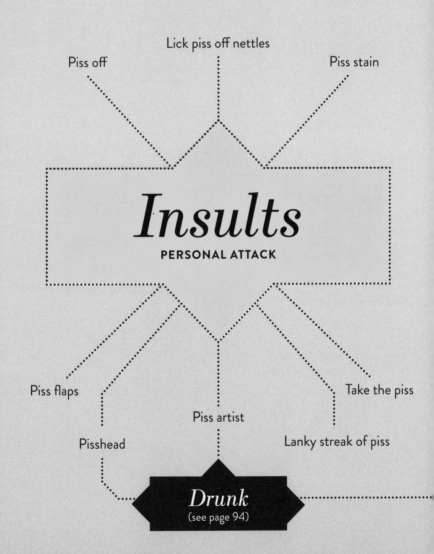

Lick piss off nettles

Piss off

Piss stain

Insults

PERSONAL ATTACK

Piss flaps

Take the piss

Piss artist

Pisshead

Lanky streak of piss

Drunk
(see page 94)

Pissing it down

The pissing rain

Precipitation

RAIN

Being pissed on

Pissed off

Anger

STRONG ANNOYANCE OR HOSTILITY

Pissed

Pissy

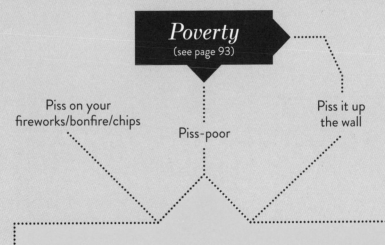

Poverty
(see page 93)

Piss on your
fireworks/bonfire/chips

Piss-poor

Piss it up
the wall

Disappointment

FAILING TO FULFILL EXPECTATIONS

Piss-take

Pisser

Piss

Piss like a racehorse

Pissing

Urinate

PASSING URINE

Piss your pants

PMSL
(Piss myself
laughing)

Defecation

Pissing out my ass

Chapter 4

{*Bollocks*}

Bollocks

A useful word to express something of poor
quality, nonsense, or the male gonads. A word
slightly less offensive than bullshit to use
when someone is talking bollocks.

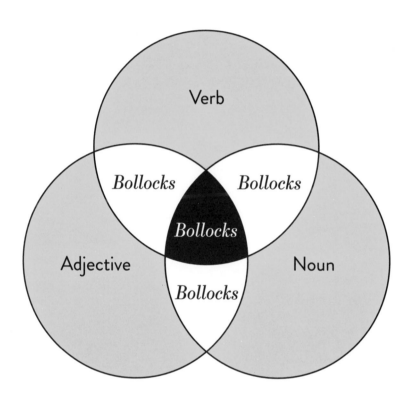

N.B. It's all bollocks.

Etymology

Bollocks derives from the Old English word for testicles, **ballokes**. The term was used in everyday language as the word for testicles and only became offensive in the mid-seventeenth century.

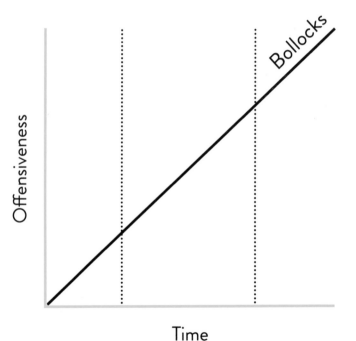

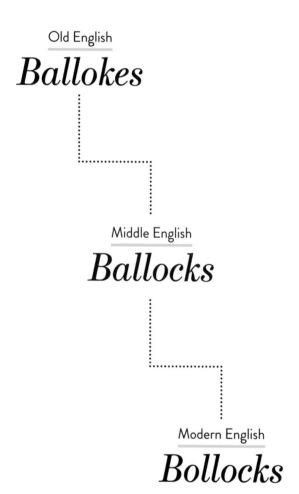

Old English

Ballokes

Middle English

Ballocks

Modern English

Bollocks

Bollocks as an Interjection, Verb, and Noun

Interjection

"Oh bollocks, I bollocked...

Verb

Noun

...him for talking bollocks out of his bollocks"

Noun

Good

DOG'S BOLLOCKS

Bad

COMPLETE BOLLOCKS

Excellent

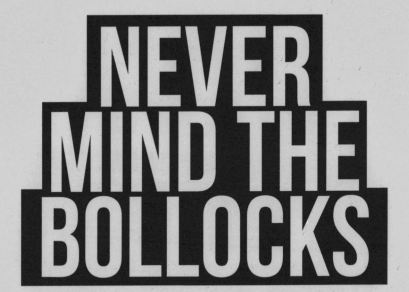

HERE'S THE SEX PISTOLS

Nevermind the Bollocks is the title of the only studio album released by the Sex Pistols, on October 28, 1977.

The band had previously appeared on live TV and famously swore at host Bill Grundy, calling him:

"You dirty sod ... You dirty old man ... You dirty bastard ... You dirty fucker ... What a fucking rotter."

Because the album's title contained the word **bollocks** it was deemed offensive. Some record charts refused to list the album. In its place was just a blank space, or in other words, bollocks all.

Breasticles and Testicles

Breasts and testes share many
euphemistic roots.

Food

Testicles	Breasts
Acorns	Apples
Grapes	Baps
Jaffas	Chest potatoes
Kiwis	Coconuts
Meatballs	Fried eggs
Nuts	Melons
Plums	Spuds
Prunes	
Spuds	
Tater tots	
Two veg	
Walnuts	

'ers

Testicles	Breasts
Conkers	Bangers
Danglers	Boulders
Knackers	Hooters
Slappers	Knockers

Spheres

Testicles	Breasts
Balls	Love orbs
Marbles	Mounds
Rocks	
Stones	

Receptacles

Testicles	Breasts
Ballbag	Fun bags
Ballsack	Jugs
Chickenskin handbag	Cans
Coin purse	
Hairy beanbag	

Nonsense

Testicles	Breasts
Goolies	Gazongas
	Yaboos
	Wabs
	Ta-Tas

Polite/Medical

Testicles	Breasts
Family jewels	Breasts
Privates	Mammaries
Testes	Bust
Scrotum	Bosoms
Gonads	Chest
Nads	

Bullshit or Bollocks?

At first glance, bullshit and bollocks seem to have a similar meaning, but there is a crucial difference.

When someone is talking bollocks, they are not aware that they are using untruths. Whereas when talking bullshit, the bullshitter is well aware that they are in fact talking bullshit.

Bullshit

"I climbed Mount Everest"

Bollocks

"Mount Everest is in Peru"

Load of bollocks

Complete bollocks

Rubbish

POOR QUALITY

Bollocksed

Bollocks!

Nevermind the
bollocks

Drunk
(see page 121)

Resignation
(see page 120)

Utter bollocks

Nonsense
FICTION

Talking bollocks

Error
(see page 123)

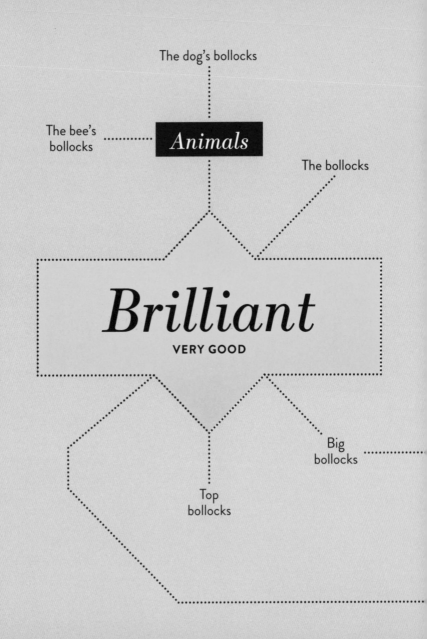

The dog's bollocks

The bee's bollocks

Animals

The bollocks

Brilliant

VERY GOOD

Top bollocks

Big bollocks

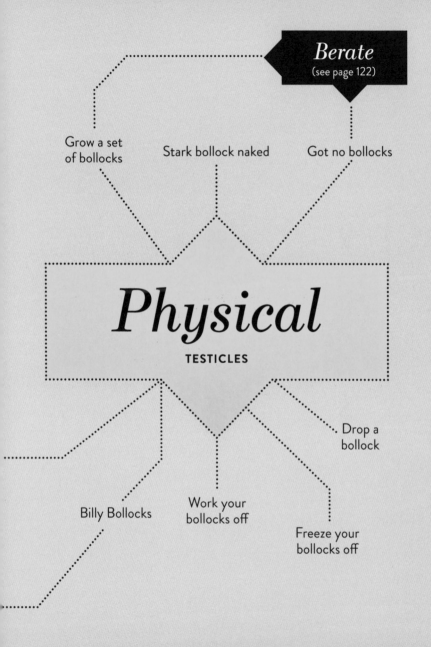

Berate
(see page 122)

Grow a set
of bollocks

Stark bollock naked

Got no bollocks

Physical

TESTICLES

Billy Bollocks

Work your
bollocks off

Freeze your
bollocks off

Drop a
bollock

Error
(see page 123)

Rubbish
(see page 116)

Bollocks!

Nonsense
(see page 117)

Resignation

**ACCEPTANCE OF SOMETHING
UNDESIRABLE BUT INEVITABLE**

Oh bollocks!

Bollocks to it

Error
(see page 123)

Rubbish
(see page 116)

Bollocksed

Drunk

INTOXICATED

Off his bollocks

A bollocking

Soppy bollocks

Berate

CRITICIZE OR REPRIMAND

Grow a set
of bollocks

Got no bollocks

Physical
(see page 119)

Drunk
(see page 121)

Rubbish
(see page 116)

Drop a bollock   Bollocksed   Bollocks up

Error

A MISTAKE

Nonsense
(see page 117)

Bollocks!

Resignation
(see page 120)

Rubbish
(see page 116)

Chapter 5

{Ass}

Ass

A person's buttocks or anus. Can also refer
to someone behaving in a silly manner.
In the UK: arse.

In the US, ass is used to describe the above
definition as well as a donkey, and it can be
interchangeable (e.g. "you're an ass"). But in the
UK, ass is mainly used to refer to donkeys.

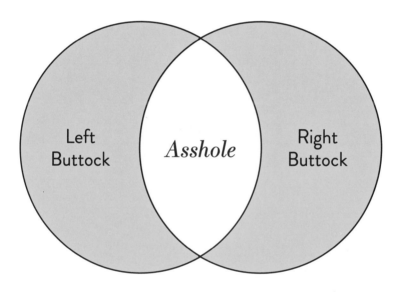

Etymology

Ass has Germanic roots and is
related closely to the modern Dutch
and German words for ass.

Lick me in the ass

Mozart, 1782

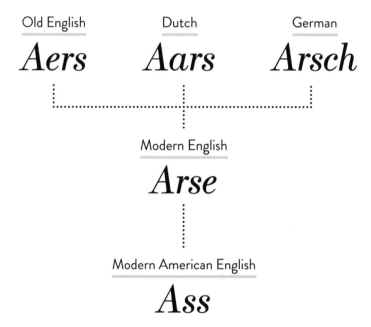

Old English
Aers

Dutch
Aars

German
Arsch

Modern English
Arse

Modern American English
Ass

Ass as an Adjective, Verb, and Noun

Adjective

"What an assy ass—he couldn't...

Noun

Verb

...be assed to look at my ass"

Noun

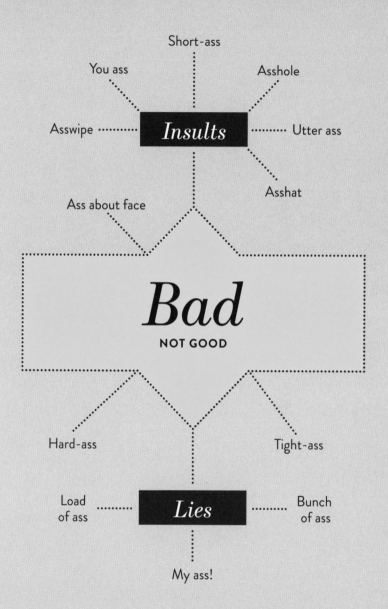

Rat ass

Drunk

INTOXICATED

Assholed

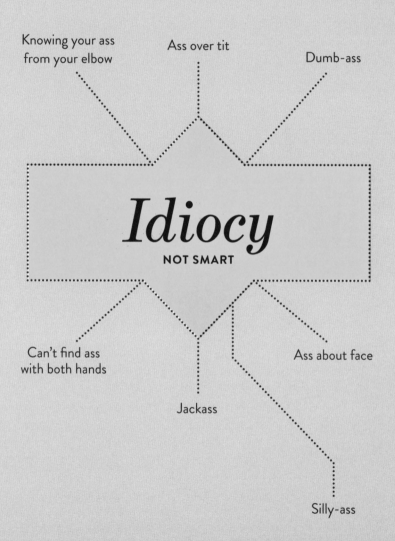

Knowing your ass from your elbow

Ass over tit

Dumb-ass

Idiocy
NOT SMART

Can't find ass with both hands

Ass about face

Jackass

Silly-ass

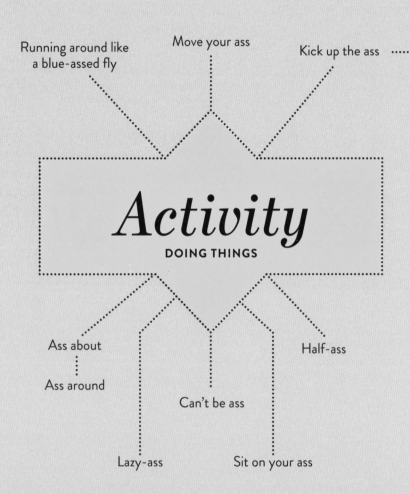

Running around like a blue-assed fly

Move your ass

Kick up the ass

Activity
DOING THINGS

Ass about

Ass around

Can't be ass

Half-ass

Lazy-ass

Sit on your ass

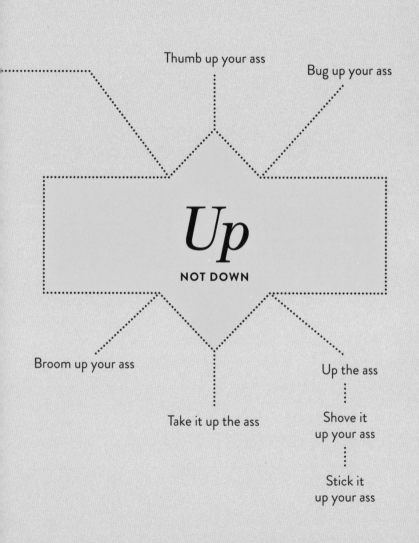

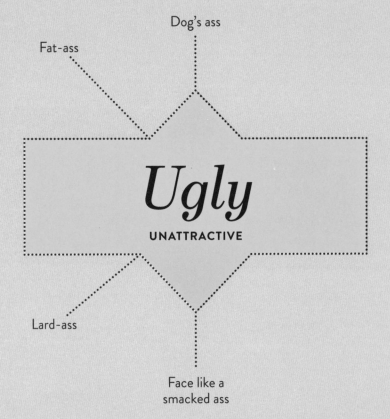

Ass biscuits

Fart-ass

Ass gravy

Fecal

POO

Ass trumpet

Ass candle

JESUS LOVES YOU

BUT I THINK YOU'RE AN ASSHOLE

Chapter 6

{*Dick*}

Dick

Dick is fairly limited in that it can refer directly to the penis, or to someone being foolish or idiotic.

Oi! My name is Dick

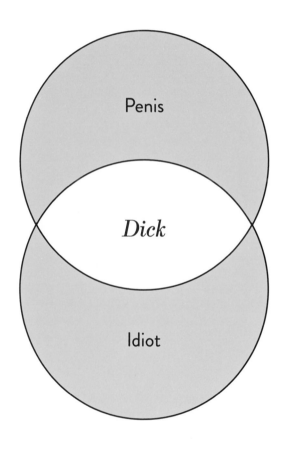

Penis

Dick

Idiot

Dick as a Verb and Noun

Noun

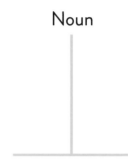

"He is such a dickhead…

Verb

...dicking around with his dick out"

Noun

Etymology

Dick is derived from the name Richard, shortened to Rick, which then became Dick. It was used to refer to an everyman, and eventually to refer to an unsavory character. It was only in the 1880s that military slang began using dick to refer to the penis.

English
Richard

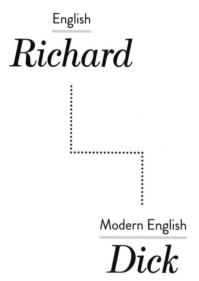

Modern English
Dick

Detective

Dick

Penis

COCK

Dickhead

Dickwad

Dicking about

Dicked over

Idiot
FOOL/FOOLING

Clever

Clever Dick

Chapter 7

{*Cunt*}

Cunt

Cunt is a vulgar word for female genitalia, also used to mean an unpleasant or stupid person.

Cunt is currently the most offensive word in the English language, and one of the last words that still has the power to shock.

London and Oxford both have a Gropecunte Lane, a former red light district. The word became taboo towards the end of the eighteenth century, and unprintable until the late twentieth century.

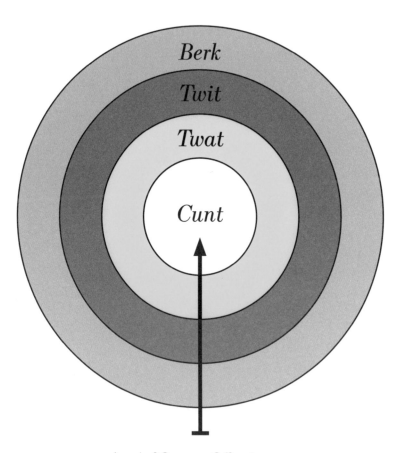

Level of Greatest Offensiveness

Cunt as an Adjective, Verb, and Noun

Adjective

"He's being a cunting cunt . . .

Noun

Verb

...because I got cunted"

Etymology

Cunt is related to **Kunta** in Norwegian and Swedish dialects and **Kunte** in German, Middle Dutch, and Danish dialects.

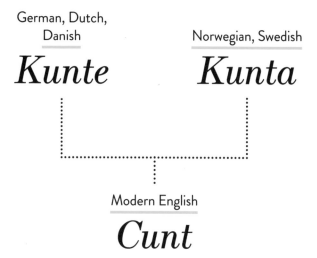

German, Dutch, Danish

Kunte

Norwegian, Swedish

Kunta

Modern English

Cunt

Genitals in the Strongest Terms

In 2016, Ofcom compiled a list of the most offensive words in the English language. Synonyms for genitalia make up most of the "strong" sections, with female genitalia dominating.

One in the pink ...

Mild

Ass

Bloody

Bugger

Cow

Crap

Damn

Ginger

Git

God

Goddam

Jesus Christ

Minger

Sod off

Medium

Asshole

Balls

Bint

Bitch

Bollocks

Bullshit

Feck

Munter

Pissed/pissed off

Shit

Son of a bitch

Tits

Strong

Bastard

Beaver

Beef curtains

Bellend

Bloodclaat

Clunge

Cock

Dick

Dickhead

Fanny

Flaps

Gash

Knob

Minge

Prick

Punani

Pussy

Snatch

Twat

Strongest

Cunt

Fuck

Motherfucker

"YOU ARE WHAT YOU EAT, I'M A CUNT"

Bernard Manning

"TRY NOT TO BE A CUNT"

Buddha

Derivations

For such a strong word, cunt has surprisingly few derivations or associated sayings. Cunty, cuntish, and cunted were only added into the *Oxford English Dictionary* in 2014.

	Usage	Meaning
Adjective	Cunty	To act like a cunt
Adjective	Cuntish	To act like a cunt
Verb	Cunted	To be drunk
Verb	Cunting	Intensify an insult

Chapter 8

{*Polite Swears*}

Polite Swears

Occasionally the circumstance may not
allow a full swear. But there are plenty of
alternatives that are safe for children's ears.

Oh fiddlesticks, I said fuck!

Root	Level 1	Level 2	Level 3
Fuck	Frick	Flip	Fiddlesticks
Shit	Crap	Shizzle	Sugar
Bollocks	Bollards	Balderdash	Blast
Dick	Cock	Knob	Pillock
Cunt	Twat	Twit	Twerp

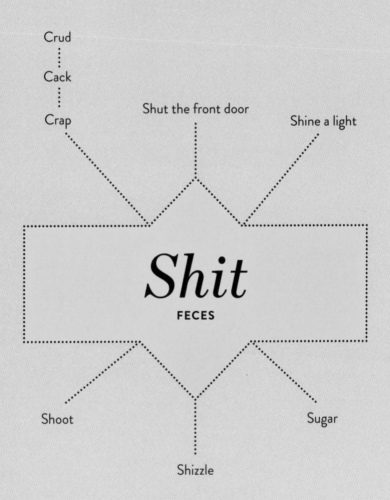

Crud

Cack

Crap

Shut the front door

Shine a light

Shit

FECES

Shoot

Sugar

Shizzle

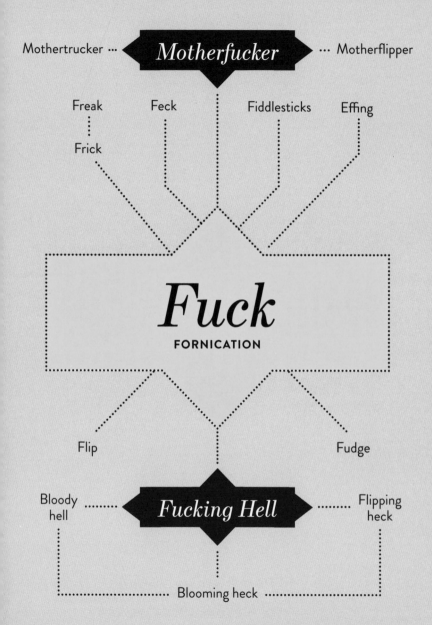

Damn

Cripes

Gor/God blimey

Blasphemy

SPEAKING SACRILEGIOUSLY

Crikey

Jesus wept

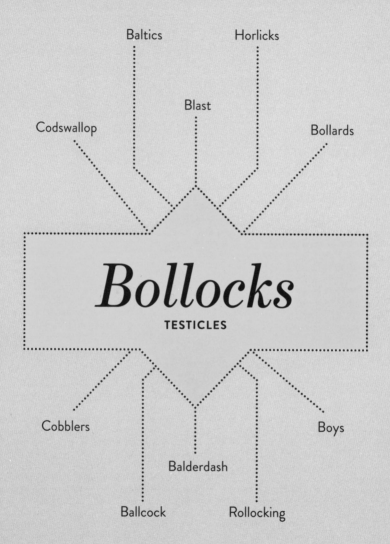

Baltics

Horlicks

Blast

Codswallop

Bollards

Bollocks

TESTICLES

Cobblers

Boys

Balderdash

Ballcock

Rollocking

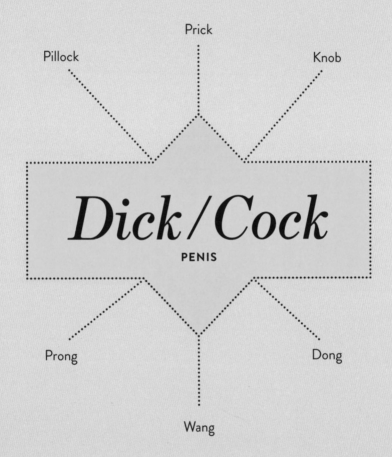

Prick

Pillock

Knob

Dick/Cock

PENIS

Prong

Dong

Wang

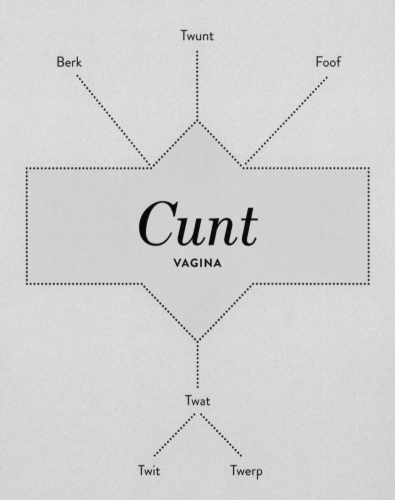

D'oh

Darn

Drat

Bugger ....

Tarnation

Exclamations

SUDDEN CRY EXPRESSING SURPRISE, STRONG EMOTION, OR PAIN

Good
Heavens

Gosh

Gordon
Bennett

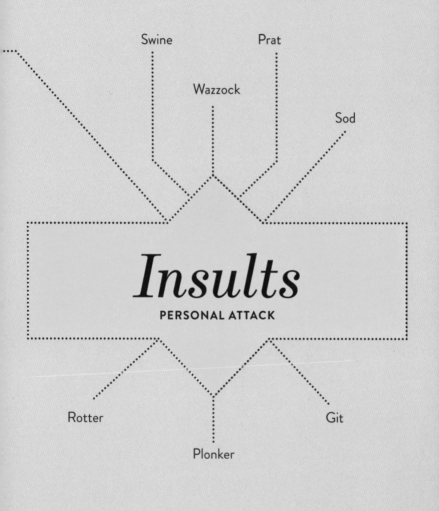

Swine

Prat

Wazzock

Sod

Insults

PERSONAL ATTACK

Rotter

Git

Plonker

Chapter 9

{*Hand Gestures*}

Hand Gestures

Obscene hand gestures are an ideal way to emphasize an insult. Or if a non-verbal insult is required (in traffic or over a large distance). Most hand gestures are sexually suggestive.

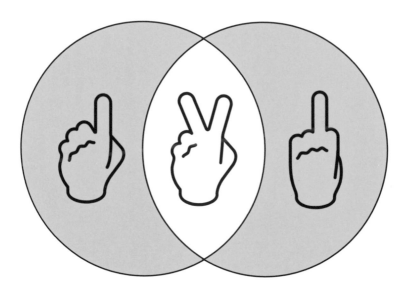

Index Finger   Middle Finger

Middle finger

To give someone the finger is equivalent to
saying **fuck off**, **fuck you,** or **up yours**.

It is performed by showing the back of a
hand and raising the middle finger.

Showing the middle finger as an insult dates back
to Ancient Greece. It represents the penis.

The bird

The finger

Flipping someone off

Two fingers

Showing two fingers is used to signify defiance (especially to authority).

To give a two finger salute, place your hand with palm facing to you and raise the index and middle finger. Now raise your hand upwards from the wrist with a flicking motion.

A common legend for the etymology of flicking the Vs is that is derives from a gesture made by English longbowmen fighting in the Battle of Agincourt. The legend states that captured bowmen had these two fingers removed so they could no longer fire their bows. Therefore, showing that you had these fingers was to demonstrate defiance. However good it sounds, there is no evidence for this origin.

Two finger salute

Flicking the Vs

The forks

Wanker

Wanker is a term that means **one who wanks** (masturbates)—also synonymous with the word tosser.

To perform the wanker sign, form your whole hand around an imaginary penis and move your hand from the wrist back and forth. For added effect you can shout "wanker!"

One variation on the wanker sign is to move the fist to the forehead, where you mime masturbating an imaginary penis. With this hand signal you are calling the target a dickhead. The second is to perform the motion in front of your mouth, miming the act of fellatio.

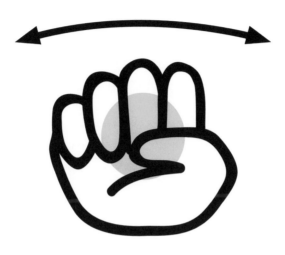

Wanker

Tosser

Dickhead
(performed on forehead)

Cocksucker
(perfomed in front of an open mouth)

Appendix 1

A list of the most commonly used words

Bottom

Anus

Ass

Asshole

Asslicker

Asswipe

Butt

Foolish

Clusterfuck

Dipshit

Douchebag

Dumbass

Fucktard

Fuckwit

Jackass

Derogatory

Bastard

Bint

Bitch

Son of a bitch

Slut

Thundercunt

Whore

Female Parts

Axewound

Beaver

Boobs

Norks

Camel toe

Clit

Clunge

Cunt

Fanny

Gash

Minge

Muff

Pussy

Pissflaps

Punani

Quim

Snatch

Tits

Twat

Tuppence

Vag

Sex Acts

Blow job

Bugger

Fellatio

Feltch

Fuck

Fuckface

Cocksucker

Handjob

Jerk off

Motherfucker

Tosspot

Tosser

Wanker

Blasphemy

Bloody

Damn

Goddamn

Jesus Christ

Male Parts

Balls

Bellend

Bollocks

Cock

Cockhead

Dick

Dickhead

Dickwad

Fuckstick

Knob

Nuts

Nutsack

Prick

Schlong

Excretions

Bullshit

Crap

Fart

Piss

Queef

Shart

Shat

Shit

Turd

Appendix 2

Getting it wrong

Breaking the rules when swearing can
be interpreted as playful improvisation.
To break the rules, use swearing not
in common use or that defies any
meaning or sense of the original words.
Ironic use like this can show you know
the rules and just don't care.

"Stick it up your balls, you queef knob"

Acknowledgements

Susan Wildish

Richard Pickles

Jake Allnutt

Simon Crotum

Jamie Stapleton

Suzanne Mathews

Walter Wildish

About the Author

Stephen Wildish is an artist, designer, and capable practitioner of the vulgar tongue. He lives in Wroughton, England.